the COCKTAIL *Bible*

A COCKTAIL FOR EVERY OCCASION

This edition published in 2011
LOVE FOOD is an imprint of Parragon Books Ltd

Parragon
Queen Street House
4 Queen Street
Bath BA1 1HE, UK

ISBN: 978-1-4454-5247-0

Printed in China

Design by Talking Design
Photography by Mike Cooper

Notes for the Reader
This book uses metric and imperial measurements. Follow the same
units of measurement throughout; do not mix metric and imperial. All
spoon measurements are level: teaspoons are assumed to be 5 ml and
tablespoons are assumed to be 15 ml. Unless otherwise stated, milk is
assumed to be full-fat and eggs are medium-size. Recipes using raw
or very lightly cooked eggs should be avoided by infants, the elderly,
pregnant and breastfeeding women, convalescents and anyone
suffering from an illness. Please consume alcohol responsibly.

CONTENTS

Introduction

Cocktails drift in and out of fashion but their appeal is always to the young or, at least, the young at heart. Making mixed drinks – even the wonderfully colourful and exotic concoctions of the contemporary cocktail bar – isn't difficult and is great fun. Reading the following basic guidelines should ensure you have all the skills of a professional bartender at your fingertips.

Bar Essentials

Cocktail shaker The standard type is a cylindrical metal container with a capacity of 500 ml/18 fl oz that has a double lid incorporating a perforated strainer. To use,

remove the lid, add ice and pour in the ingredients listed in the recipe. Close securely and shake vigorously for 10–20 seconds, until the outside of the shaker is frosted with a fine mist. Remove the small lid and pour the cocktail into the appropriate glass. If your cocktail shaker doesn't have an integral strainer, you will need a separate one. The Boston shaker consists of double conical containers and is designed to be used with a Hawthorn strainer. It's best not to mix more than 2 servings of a cocktail at a time.

Mixing glass This is used for making clear cocktails. It need be no more complicated than the container of your cocktail shaker or a jug about the same size, but you can also buy a professional mixing glass. To use, add ice, pour in the ingredients listed in the recipe and stir vigorously for 20 seconds. Strain into the appropriate glass.

Strainer A bar strainer or Hawthorn strainer is the perfect tool to prevent ice and other unwanted ingredients from being poured from the shaker or mixing glass into the serving glass. You could also use a small nylon sieve.

Jigger Also called a measure, this small measuring cup is often double-ended and shaped like an hourglass. Standard metric jiggers are 25 ml and 35 ml, while imperial jiggers are 1 fl oz and 1½ fl oz, representing 1 and 1½ measures respectively. The proportions of the various ingredients, but not the specific quantities, are critical, so if you don't have a jigger, you can use the small lid of your cocktail shaker, or a liqueur, schnapps or shot glass, or even a small egg cup.

Bar spoon This long-handled spoon is used for stirring cocktails in a mixing glass.

Muddler This is simply a miniature masher used for crushing ingredients, such as herbs and sugar, in the base of a glass. You can also use a mortar and pestle or even the back of a spoon.

Other basics Lots of ordinary kitchen equipment is useful: 1 or more corkscrews, cocktail sticks,

citrus juicer or reamer, chopping board, some paring, kitchen and canelle knives, a citrus zester, a selection of jugs and a blender for creamy cocktails and slushes. You will also require an ice bucket and tongs – never pick up ice with your fingers. Optional extras include swizzle sticks and straws.

Glasses
Champagne flute Tall thin stemmed glass holding 125–150 ml/ 4–5 fl oz.

Cocktail glass Stemmed glass with a cone-shaped bowl holding 125–150 ml/4–5 fl oz.

Collins glass Tall, narrow glass with straight sides, usually holding 300 ml/10 fl oz.

Goblet Short-stemmed glass with a large bowl holding 300 ml/10 fl oz.

Highball glass Tall, straight glass holding 225 ml/8 fl oz.

Margarita glass Stemmed glass with a small bowl topped with a wide saucer shape.

Old-fashioned glass Chunky glass holding 225 ml/8 fl oz.

Shot glass Small glass holding 50 ml/2 fl oz, suitable for shooters.

Bartender's Tips

Sugar syrup Even fine caster sugar often fails to dissolve completely in the brief time that a cocktail is shaken or stirred, so it is better to use sugar syrup or syrop de gomme when sweetening drinks. To make this, put 4 tablespoons caster sugar and 4 tablespoons water into a small saucepan. Gradually bring to the boil over a low heat, stirring constantly until the sugar has dissolved. Boil, without stirring, for 1–2 minutes, then and leave to cool. Store in a sterilized jar or bottle in the refrigerator for up to 2 months.

Chilling For absolute perfection you should chill spirits, mixers and serving glasses in the refrigerator. However, it's not always possible to find room for glasses and you should never put fine crystal in the refrigerator. As an alternative, fill glasses with cracked ice, stir well, then tip out the ice and any water before pouring in the cocktail.

Frosting glasses You can use caster sugar, fine salt or desiccated coconut to decorate the rim of a glass. Rub the rim with a little lemon or lime juice and then dip the glass upside down into a shallow saucer containing your chosen decoration.

Layering (pousse-café) To make a multi-layered drink, slowly pour the liqueurs or spirits, in the order specified in the recipe, over the back of a teaspoon into the glass. Each layer then settles on top of the layer before it.

Ice To crack ice, put cubes in a strong plastic bag and hit with the smooth side of a meat mallet or a rolling pin. Alternatively, bang the bag against a wall. Ice can be crushed in a food processor or blender. To store large quantities of ice, place the cubes in a strong plastic bag and before returning them to the freezer squirt with soda water to stop the cubes from sticking together.

The Classics

Martini

FOR MANY, THIS IS THE ULTIMATE COCKTAIL. IT IS NAMED AFTER ITS
INVENTOR, MARTINI DE ANNA DE TOGGIA, NOT THE FAMOUS BRAND
OF VERMOUTH!

SERVES 1
3 measures gin
1 tsp dry vermouth, or to taste
cracked ice cubes
green cocktail olive, to
  decorate

1 Shake the gin and
  vermouth over cracked
  ice until well frosted.
2 Strain into a chilled
  cocktail glass and dress
  with the cocktail olive.

Daiquiri

DAIQUIRI IS A TOWN IN CUBA, WHERE THIS DRINK WAS SAID TO HAVE
BEEN INVENTED IN THE EARLY PART OF THE TWENTIETH CENTURY. A
BUSINESSMAN HAD RUN OUT OF IMPORTED GIN AND SO HAD TO MAKE
DO WITH THE LOCAL DRINK – RUM – WHICH, AT THAT TIME, WAS OFTEN
OF UNRELIABLE QUALITY.

SERVES 1
2 measures white rum
¾ measure lime juice
½ tsp sugar syrup
cracked ice

1 Pour the rum, lime
  juice and sugar syrup
  over ice and shake
  vigorously until well
  frosted.
2 Strain into a chilled
  cocktail glass.

Manhattan

SAID TO HAVE BEEN INVENTED BY SIR WINSTON CHURCHILL'S AMERICAN MOTHER, JENNIE, THE MANHATTAN IS ONE OF MANY COCKTAILS NAMED AFTER PLACES IN NEW YORK.

SERVES 1
dash Angostura bitters
3 measures rye whisky
1 measure sweet vermouth
cracked ice cubes
cocktail cherry, to decorate

1 Shake the liquids over cracked ice in a mixing glass and mix well.
2 Strain into a chilled glass and decorate with the cherry.

Sangria

A PERFECT LONG COLD DRINK FOR A CROWD OF FRIENDS AT A
SUMMER BARBECUE!

SERVES 6
juice of 1 orange
juice of 1 lemon
2 tbsp caster sugar
ice cubes
1 orange, thinly sliced
1 lemon, thinly sliced
1 bottle red wine, chilled
lemonade

1 Shake the orange and
  lemon juice with the
  sugar and transfer to a
  large bowl or jug.
2 When the sugar has
  dissolved, add a few
  ice cubes, sliced fruit
  and wine.
3 Marinate for 1 hour if
  possible, and then add
  lemonade to taste and
  more ice.

Mimosa

SO CALLED BECAUSE IT RESEMBLES THE COLOUR OF A MIMOSA'S
ATTRACTIVE YELLOW BLOOM.

SERVES 1
flesh of 1 passion fruit
½ measure orange Curaçao
crushed ice
champagne, chilled
slice of star fruit, to decorate

1 Scoop out the passion
   fruit flesh into a jug
   or shaker and shake
   with the Curaçao and
   a little crushed ice until
   frosted.
2 Pour into the base
   of a champagne
   flute and top up with
   champagne.
3 Decorate with the slice
   of star fruit.

Bellini

THIS DELICIOUS CONCOCTION WAS CREATED BY GIUSEPPE CIPRIANI AT HARRY'S BAR IN VENICE, AROUND 1943.

SERVES 1

1 measure fresh peach juice made from lightly sweetened liquidized peaches
caster sugar
3 measures champagne, chilled

1 Dip the rim of a champagne flute into some peach juice and then into the sugar to create a sugar-frosted effect. Set aside to dry. Chill.
2 Pour the peach juice into the chilled flute and stir gently.
3 Top up with champagne.

Margarita

THIS COCKTAIL, ATTRIBUTED TO FRANCISCO MORALES AND INVENTED IN 1942 IN MEXICO, IS A MORE CIVILIZED VERSION OF THE ORIGINAL WAY TO DRINK TEQUILA – A LICK OF SALT FROM THE BACK OF YOUR HAND, A SUCK OF LIME JUICE AND A SHOT OF TEQUILA!

SERVES 1
lime wedge
coarse salt
3 measures white tequila
1 measure Triple Sec or
    Cointreau
2 measures lime juice
cracked ice cubes
slice of lime, to decorate

1 Rub the rim of a chilled cocktail glass with the lime wedge and then dip in a saucer of coarse salt to frost.

2 Shake the tequila, Triple Sec and lime juice vigorously over cracked ice until well frosted.

3 Strain into the prepared glass and decorate with the slice of lime.

Club Mojito

DARK RUM IS RICH IN FLAVOUR AND REDOLENT OF SUNSHINE HOLIDAY MEMORIES.

SERVES 1
1 tsp syrop de gomme
few mint leaves, plus extra
   to decorate
juice ½ lime
ice
2 measures Jamaican rum
soda water
dash Angostura bitters

1 Put the syrop, mint leaves and lime juice into a glass and muddle the mint leaves.
2 Add the ice and rum and shake well, pour into a cocktail glass and top up with soda water to taste.
3 Finish with a dash of Angostura bitters and decorate with the remaining mint leaves.

Mai Tai

CREATED IN 1944 BY RESTAURATEUR 'TRADER VIC' IT WAS DESCRIBED AS 'MAI TAI – ROE AE' MEANING 'OUT OF THIS WORLD'. IT IS ALWAYS FLAMBOYANTLY DRESSED.

SERVES 1
2 measures white rum
2 measures dark rum
1 measure orange Curaçao
1 measure lime juice
1 tbsp orgeat
1 tbsp grenadine
cracked ice cubes
slices of pineapple, pieces
    of fruit peel, cocktail
    cherries and straws, to
    decorate

1 Shake the white and dark rums, Curaçao, lime juice, orgeat and grenadine vigorously over ice until well frosted.

2 Strain into a chilled glass and decorate as you wish.

The New Wave

Mudslide

DESPITE ITS OMINOUS-SOUNDING NAME, THIS IS A RICHLY FLAVOURED CREAMY CONCOCTION THAT IS DELICIOUS WHATEVER THE WEATHER.

SERVES 1
1½ measures Kahlúa
1½ measures Baileys Irish
  Cream
1½ measures vodka
cracked ice cubes

1 Shake the Kahlúa, Baileys Irish Cream and vodka vigorously over ice until well frosted.
2 Strain into a chilled glass.

Mint Julep

A JULEP IS SIMPLY A MIXED DRINK SWEETENED WITH SYRUP. THE MINT JULEP WAS PROBABLY FIRST MADE IN THE UNITED STATES, AND IS THE TRADITIONAL DRINK OF THE KENTUCKY DERBY.

SERVES 1
leaves from 1 fresh mint sprig,
  plus extra to decorate
1 tbsp sugar syrup
crushed ice cubes
3 measures bourbon whiskey

1 Put the mint leaves and sugar syrup into a small chilled glass and mash with a teaspoon.
2 Add the crushed ice and shake to mix, before adding the bourbon.
3 Decorate with the remaining mint leaves.

White Lady

SIMPLE, ELEGANT, SUBTLE AND MUCH MORE POWERFUL THAN APPEARANCE SUGGESTS, THIS IS THE PERFECT COCKTAIL TO SERVE BEFORE AN AL FRESCO SUMMER DINNER.

SERVES 1
2 measures gin
1 measure Triple Sec
1 measure lemon juice
cracked ice cubes

1 Shake the gin, Triple Sec and lemon juice vigorously over ice until well frosted.
2 Strain into a chilled cocktail glass.

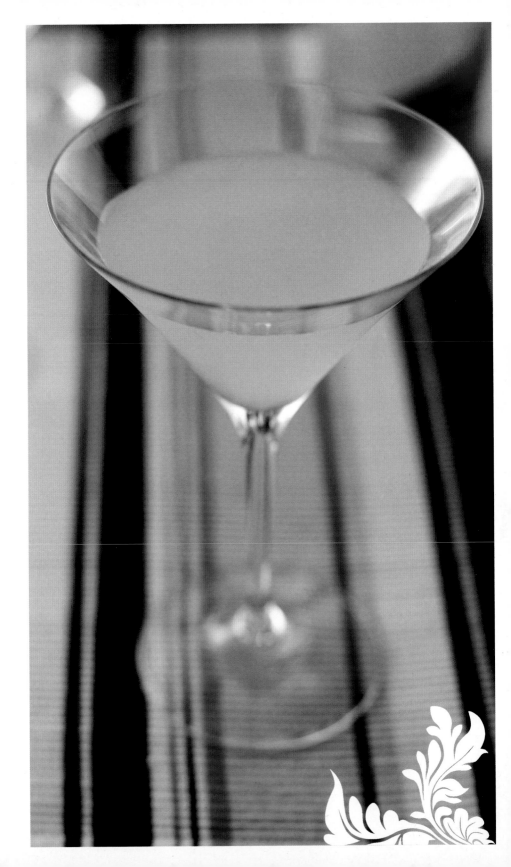

Kamikaze

NO TURNING BACK ON THIS ONE. IT'S SO DELICIOUS – YOU WON'T BE
ABLE TO PUT IT DOWN!

SERVES 1
1 measure vodka
1 measure Triple Sec
½ measure fresh lime juice
½ measure fresh lemon juice
ice
dry white wine, chilled
pieces of lime and
   cucumber, to decorate

1 Shake the first four
   ingredients together
   over ice until well
   frosted.
2 Strain into a chilled
   glass and top up with
   wine.
3 Dress with the lime and
   cucumber.

Black Widow

NOT AS WICKED AS ITS TITLE SUGGESTS, BUT IF YOU ARE FEELING
ADVENTUROUS YOU COULD TAKE IT STRAIGHT, ON THE ROCKS!

SERVES 1
⅔ measure dark rum
⅓ measure Southern
  Comfort
juice ½ lime
dash Curaçao
ice
soda water
lime peel, to decorate

1 Shake the first four
  ingredients together
  well over ice and strain
  into a chilled tumbler.
2 Top up with soda water
  to taste and decorate
  with the lime peel.

Indian Summer

THE COFFEE LIQUEUR IS THE KEY INGREDIENT IN THIS DELICIOUS LONG MIX – IT WOULD BE GOOD WITH CRÈME DE NOYEAU OR CRÈME DE CACAO, TOO.

SERVES 1
1 measure vodka
2 measures Kahlúa
1 measure gin
2 measures pineapple juice
ice
tonic water

1 Shake the first four ingredients well over ice until frosted.
2 Strain into a medium cocktail glass or wine glass and top up with tonic water to taste.

Ocean Breeze

IT'S A BREEZE TO MAKE AND AS COLOURFUL AS THE WHIPPED-UP
OCEAN ON AN EARLY MORNING. JUST DON'T DILUTE IT TOO MUCH.

SERVES 1
1 measure white rum
1 measure amaretto
½ measure blue Curaçao
½ measure pineapple juice
crushed ice
soda water

1 Shake the first four
  ingredients together
  over ice.
2 Pour into a tall glass
  and top up with soda
  water to taste.

Whiskey Sour

ORIGINATING IN THE AMERICAN SOUTH AND USING SOME OF THE BEST
AMERICAN WHISKEY, THIS CLASSIC CAN ALSO BE MADE WITH VODKA,
GIN OR OTHER SPIRITS.

SERVES 1
1 measure lemon or lime
   juice
2 measures blended whiskey
1 tsp caster sugar or syrop
   de gomme
ice
slice of lime or lemon, to
   decorate
maraschino cherry, to
   decorate

1 Shake the first three
   ingredients well over
   ice and strain into a
   cocktail glass.
2 Decorate with the slice
   of lime or lemon, and
   the cherry.

The Perfect Pick-Me-Up

White Cosmopolitan

NOTHING LIKE ITS PINK COUSIN THE COSMOPOLITAN, FOR THIS IS FAR MORE FRUITY AND, INSTEAD OF VODKA, IT IS BASED ON A PUNCHY LEMON-FLAVOURED LIQUEUR.

SERVES 1
1½ measures limoncello
½ measure Cointreau
1 measure white cranberry
   and grape juice
ice
dash orange bitters
few red cranberries, to
   decorate

1 Shake the first three ingredients over ice until frosted.
2 Strain into a chilled cocktail glass.
3 Add a dash of bitters and dress with the cranberries.

Pink Squirrel

CRÈME DE NOYEAU HAS A WONDERFUL, SLIGHTLY BITTER, NUTTY FLAVOUR BUT IS, IN FACT, MADE FROM PEACH AND APRICOT KERNELS. IT IS USUALLY SERVED AS A LIQUEUR, BUT DOES COMBINE WELL WITH SOME OTHER INGREDIENTS IN COCKTAILS.

SERVES 1
2 measures dark crème de cacao
1 measure crème de noyeau
1 measure single cream
cracked ice cubes

1 Shake the crème de cacao, crème de noyeau and single cream vigorously over ice until well frosted.
2 Strain into a chilled cocktail glass.

Deauville Passion

DEAUVILLE WAS ELEGANT, EXTRAVAGANT AND VERY FASHIONABLE DURING THE COCKTAIL ERA EARLY LAST CENTURY AND NO DOUBT MANY GREAT COCKTAILS WERE CREATED THERE.

SERVES 1
1¾ measures cognac
1¼ measures apricot
    Curaçao
1¼ measures passion-fruit
    juice
ice
bitter lemon, to taste
mint leaves, to decorate

1 Shake the first three
    ingredients over ice
    until well frosted.
2 Strain into a chilled
    glass and top up with
    the bitter lemon, to
    taste.
3 Decorate with the mint
    leaves.

Zombie

THE INDIVIDUAL INGREDIENTS OF THIS COCKTAIL, INCLUDING LIQUEURS AND FRUIT JUICES, VARY CONSIDERABLY FROM ONE RECIPE TO ANOTHER, BUT ALL ZOMBIES CONTAIN A MIXTURE OF WHITE, GOLDEN AND DARK RUM IN A RANGE OF PROPORTIONS.

SERVES 1
2 measures dark rum
2 measures white rum
1 measure golden rum
1 measure Triple Sec
1 measure lime juice
1 measure orange juice
1 measure pineapple juice
1 measure guava juice
1 tbsp grenadine
1 tbsp orgeat
1 tsp Pernod
crushed ice cubes
sprigs of fresh mint and
  pineapple wedges, to
  decorate

1 Shake all the liquids together over crushed ice until smooth.
2 Pour, without straining, into a chilled glass.
3 Decorate with the mint and the pineapple wedges.

Adam 'n' Eve

DON'T EXPECT THIS COCKTAIL TO BE FULL OF APPLES! THE BASE IS SHARP AND ASTRINGENT, WHILST THE TOP IS SWEET AND FROTHY – NO DISCRIMINATION HERE, OF COURSE!

SERVES 1

2 measures Triple Sec
1 measure vodka
1 measure grapefruit juice
1 measure cranberry juice
ice
5-6 cubes pineapple
2 tsp caster sugar
crushed ice
slice of strawberry, to decorate

1 Shake the first four ingredients over ice until well frosted.
2 Strain into a chilled glass.
3 In a blender, whizz the pineapple with sugar and 1–2 tbsp of crushed ice to a frothy slush.
4 Float gently on the top of the cocktail.
5 Dress with a slice of strawberry.

Orange Blossom

DURING THE PROHIBITION YEARS IN THE USA, GIN WAS OFTEN QUITE LITERALLY MADE IN THE BATHTUB AND FLAVOURED WITH FRESH ORANGE JUICE TO CONCEAL ITS FILTHY FLAVOUR. MADE WITH GOOD-QUALITY GIN, WHICH NEEDS NO SUCH CONCEALMENT, THIS DRINK IS DELIGHTFULLY REFRESHING.

SERVES 1
2 measures gin
2 measures orange juice
cracked ice cubes
slice of orange, to decorate

1 Shake the gin and orange juice vigorously over ice until well frosted.
2 Strain into a chilled cocktail glass and decorate with the orange slice.

Moonlight

THIS LIGHT WINE-BASED COCKTAIL IS AN IDEAL DRINK TO MAKE FOR
SEVERAL PEOPLE.

SERVES 4
3 measures grapefruit juice
4 measures gin
1 measure kirsch
4 measures white wine
½ tsp lemon zest
ice

1 Shake the first five
ingredients well over
ice and strain into
chilled glasses.

Cherry Kitch

THIS IS A VELVETY SMOOTH COCKTAIL, FRUITY BUT WITH A RICH BRANDY UNDERTONE. A TOUCH OF MARASCHINO LIQUEUR ADDED AT THE END WOULD BE GOOD, TOO.

SERVES 1
1 measure cherry brandy
2 measures pineapple juice
½ measure kirsch
1 egg white
1 scoop crushed ice
frozen maraschino cherry, to
  decorate

1 Shake the first four ingredients well over ice until frosted.
2 Pour into a chilled tall thin glass and decorate with the frozen maraschino cherry.

Renaissance

Cosmopolitan

INVITING AND REFRESHING, THE COSMOPOLITAN IS THE BEVERAGE OF CHOICE FOR THE 'SEX AND THE CITY' GIRLS AND IS A MUST AT ANY FASHIONABLE PARTY.

SERVES 1
2 measures vodka
1 measure Triple Sec
1 measure fresh lime juice
1 measure cranberry juice
ice
strip of orange peel

1 Shake all the liquid ingredients over ice until well frosted.
2 Strain into a chilled cocktail glass.
3 Dress with the strip of orange peel.

Sex On The Beach

HOLIDAY DRINKS ARE OFTEN LONG AND FRUITY AND THIS REFRESHING
COCKTAIL IS REMINISCENT OF HAPPY DAYS IN THE SUN.

SERVES 1
1 measure peach schnapps
1 measure vodka
2 measures fresh orange juice
3 measures cranberry and
  peach juice
ice and crushed ice
dash of lemon juice
piece of orange peel, to
  decorate

1 Shake the first four
  ingredients over ice
  until well frosted.
2 Strain into a glass
  filled with crushed iced
  and squeeze over the
  lemon juice.
3 Dress with the orange
  peel.

Harvey Wallbanger

THIS WELL-KNOWN CONTEMPORARY CLASSIC COCKTAIL IS A GREAT PARTY DRINK – MIX IT STRONG AT FIRST, THEN WEAKER AS THE EVENING GOES BY – OR WITHOUT ALCOHOL FOR DRIVERS AND NO ONE WOULD KNOW!

SERVES 1
ice cubes
3 measures vodka
8 measures orange juice
2 tsp Galliano
cherry and slice of orange,
  to decorate

1 Half fill a glass with ice, pour vodka and orange over the ice cubes, and float Galliano on top.
2 Garnish with the cherry and the slice of orange.
3 For a warming variant, mix a splash of ginger wine with the vodka and orange.

Bloody Mary

THIS CLASSIC COCKTAIL WAS INVENTED IN 1921 AT THE LEGENDARY HARRY'S BAR IN PARIS. THERE ARE NUMEROUS VERSIONS – SOME MUCH HOTTER AND SPICIER THAN OTHERS. INGREDIENTS MAY INCLUDE HORSERADISH SAUCE IN ADDITION TO OR INSTEAD OF TABASCO SAUCE.

SERVES 1
dash Tabasco sauce
dash Worcestershire sauce
cracked ice cubes
2 measures vodka
splash dry sherry
6 measures tomato juice
juice ½ lemon
pinch celery salt
pinch cayenne pepper
celery stick with leaves, to
    decorate
slice of lemon, to decorate

1 Dash the Worcestershire sauce and Tabasco sauce over ice in a shaker and add the vodka, splash of dry sherry, tomato juice and lemon juice.
2 Shake vigorously until frosted.
3 Strain into a tall chilled glass, add a pinch of celery salt and a pinch of cayenne and decorate with the celery stick and the slice of lemon.

Slow Comfortable Screw

ALWAYS USE FRESHLY SQUEEZED ORANGE JUICE TO MAKE THIS
REFRESHING COCKTAIL – IT IS JUST NOT THE SAME WITH BOTTLED
JUICE. THIS SIMPLE, CLASSIC COCKTAIL HAS GIVEN RISE TO NUMEROUS
AND INCREASINGLY ELABORATE VARIATIONS.

SERVES 1
2 measures sloe gin
orange juice
cracked ice cubes
slice of orange, to decorate

1 Shake the sloe gin
and orange juice over
ice until well frosted
and pour into a chilled
glass.
2 Decorate with the slice
of orange.

Long Island Iced Tea

DATING BACK TO THE DAYS OF THE AMERICAN PROHIBITION, WHEN IT WAS DRUNK OUT OF CUPS IN AN ATTEMPT TO FOOL THE FBI THAT IT WAS HARMLESS, THIS COCKTAIL HAS EVOLVED FROM THE ORIGINAL SIMPLE COMBINATION OF VODKA WITH A DASH OF COLA!

SERVES 1

2 measures vodka
1 measure gin
1 measure white tequila
1 measure white rum
½ measure white crème de menthe
2 measures lemon juice
1 tsp sugar syrup
cracked ice cubes
cola
slice of lime or lemon, to decorate

1 Shake the vodka, gin, tequila, rum, crème de menthe, lemon juice and sugar syrup vigorously over ice until well frosted.
2 Strain into an ice-filled glass and top up with cola.
3 Dress with the lime or lemon slice.

Screwdriver

THIS COCKTAIL HAS UNIVERSAL APPEAL, AND IS GREAT TO SERVE TO GUESTS AT A PARTY IF YOU ARE NOT SURE OF INDIVIDUAL TASTES. FRESHLY SQUEEZED ORANGE JUICE IS A MUST.

SERVES 1
cracked ice cubes
2 measures vodka
orange juice
slice of orange, to decorate

1 Fill a chilled glass with cracked ice cubes.
2 Pour the vodka over the ice and top up with orange juice.
3 Stir well to mix and dress with the slice of orange.

Seabreeze

PINK GRAPEFRUIT JUICE IS MUCH SWEETER AND SUBTLER THAN ITS PALER COUSIN, SO IT IS IDEAL TO MIX IN COCKTAILS WHERE YOU WANT JUST A SLIGHT SHARPNESS.

SERVES 1
1½ measures vodka
½ measure cranberry juice
ice
pink grapefruit juice, to taste

1 Shake the vodka and cranberry juice over ice until frosted.
2 Pour into a chilled tumbler or long glass and top up with pink grapefruit juice to taste.

Black Russian

HISTORY RECORDS ONLY WHITE AND RED RUSSIANS. THE OMISSION OF THE BLACK RUSSIAN IS A SAD OVERSIGHT. FOR A COFFEE LIQUEUR, YOU CAN USE EITHER TIA MARIA OR KAHLÚA, DEPENDING ON YOUR PERSONAL TASTE – THE LATTER IS SWEETER.

SERVES 1
2 measures vodka
1 measure coffee liqueur
4-6 cracked ice cubes

1 Pour the vodka and liqueur over cracked ice cubes in a small chilled glass.
2 Stir to mix.

Innovative

Blue Monday

THE LOVELY COLOUR AND FRUITY FLAVOUR OF THIS COCKTAIL IS
GUARANTEED TO MAKE MONDAY YOUR FAVOURITE DAY OF THE WEEK.

SERVES 1
cracked ice
1 measure vodka
½ measure Cointreau
1 tbsp blue Curaçao

1 Put the cracked ice
   into a mixing glass or
   jug and pour in the
   vodka, Cointreau and
   Curaçao.
2 Stir well and strain into
   a cocktail glass.

Fuzzy Navel

THIS IS ANOTHER COCKTAIL WITH A NAME THAT PLAYS ON THE
INGREDIENTS – FUZZY TO REMIND YOU THAT IT CONTAINS PEACH
SCHNAPPS AND NAVEL BECAUSE IT IS MIXED WITH ORANGE JUICE.

SERVES 1
2 measures vodka
1 measure peach schnapps
250ml/9 fl oz orange juice
cracked ice cubes
physalis (cape gooseberry),
  to decorate

1 Shake the vodka,
peach schnapps and
orange juice vigorously
over cracked ice until
well frosted.
2 Strain into a chilled
cocktail glass and
decorate with the
physalis.

Golden Frog

AS A RULE, CLASSIC VODKA COCKTAILS WERE INTENDED TO PROVIDE
AN ALCOHOLIC DRINK WITH NO TELL-TALE SIGNS ON THE BREATH AND
WERE USUALLY FAIRLY SIMPLE MIXES OF NON-ALCOHOLIC FLAVOURS.
CONTEMPORARY VODKA COCKTAILS OFTEN INCLUDE OTHER SPIRITS.

SERVES 1
ice cubes
1 measure vodka
1 measure Strega
1 measure Galliano
1 measure lemon juice

1 Whizz 4–6 ice cubes
   in a blender with the
   vodka, Strega, Galliano
   and lemon juice.
2 Blend until slushy.
3 Pour into a chilled
   cocktail glass.

Moscow Mule

THIS COCKTAIL CAME INTO EXISTENCE THROUGH A HAPPY
COINCIDENCE DURING THE 1930S. AN AMERICAN BAR OWNER HAD
OVERSTOCKED GINGER BEER AND A REPRESENTATIVE OF A SOFT
DRINKS COMPANY INVENTED THE MOSCOW MULE TO HELP HIM OUT.

SERVES 1
2 measures vodka
1 measure lime juice
cracked ice cubes
ginger beer
slice of lime, to decorate

1 Shake the vodka and
lime juice vigorously
over ice until well
frosted.
2 Half-fill a chilled
cocktail glass with
cracked ice cubes and
strain the cocktail over
them.
3 Top up with ginger
beer. Dress with the
slice of lime.

Peartini

WHILE LESS POPULAR THAN PEACH OR CHERRY EAU DE VIE, PEAR BRANDY HAS A DELICATE FRAGRANCE AND LOVELY FLAVOUR, BUT DON'T CONFUSE IT WITH PEAR LIQUEUR.

SERVES 1
1 tsp caster sugar
pinch of ground cinnamon
1 lemon wedge
cracked ice
1 measure vodka
1 measure pear brandy, such
 as Poire William or Pera
 Segnana

1 Mix together the sugar and cinnamon on a saucer. Rub the outside rim of a cocktail glass with the lemon wedge, then dip it into the sugar and cinnamon mixture. Set aside.

2 Put the cracked ice into a mixing glass or jug and pour in the vodka and pear brandy. Stir well and strain into the prepared glass, without disturbing the frosting.

Salty Dog

WHEN THIS COCKTAIL FIRST APPEARED, GIN-BASED MIXES WERE BY FAR THE MOST POPULAR, BUT NOWADAYS A SALTY DOG IS MORE FREQUENTLY MADE WITH VODKA. CHOOSE WHICHEVER YOU PREFER, BUT THE COCKTAILS WILL HAVE DIFFERENT FLAVOURS.

SERVES 1
1 tbsp granulated sugar
1 tbsp coarse salt
lemon half
6-8 cracked ice cubes
2 measures vodka
grapefruit juice

1 Mix the sugar and salt in a saucer. Rub the rim of a chilled cocktail glass with the lemon half, then dip it in the sugar and salt mixture to frost.
2 Fill the glass with cracked ice cubes and pour the vodka over them.
3 Top up with grapefruit juice and stir to mix. Drink with a straw.

Spotted Bikini

A CHEEKY NAME FOR AN AMUSING COCKTAIL. IT ALSO TASTES GREAT,
ALTHOUGH YOU MAY LIKE TO ADD A LITTLE SUGAR TO TASTE.

SERVES 1
2 measures vodka
1 measure white rum
1 measure cold milk
juice ½ lemon
ice
1 ripe passion fruit
piece of lemon, to decorate

1 Shake the first four
   ingredients over ice
   until well frosted.
2 Strain into a chilled
   medium cocktail glass
   and add the passion
   fruit, not strained, at
   the last minute so you
   see the black seeds.
3 Dress with the piece of
   lemon.

Woo-woo

BE SURE TO WOO YOUR FRIENDS WITH THIS REFRESHING AND SIMPLE
DRINK. IT'S ALSO GREAT FOR PARTIES.

SERVES 1
cracked ice cubes
2 measures vodka
2 measures peach schnapps
4 measures cranberry juice
physalis (cape gooseberry), to
   decorate

1 Half-fill a chilled
   cocktail glass with
   cracked ice.
2 Pour the vodka, peach
   and cranberry juice
   over the ice.
3 Stir well to mix and
   decorate with the
   physalis.

In Vogue

Vodkatini

A CERTAIN MR BOND POPULARISED THE USE OF VODKA AS THE BASE OF THE MARTINI, RATHER THAN GIN, HENCE THE VODKATINI IS NOW WIDELY ACCEPTED AS AN INCREDIBLY STYLISH AND TASTY ALTERNATIVE.

SERVES 1
1 measure vodka
ice
dash dry vermouth
a twist of lemon peel or a
single olive, to decorate

1 Pour the vodka over a handful of ice in a mixing glass.
2 Add the vermouth, stir well and strain into a cocktail glass.
3 Dress with the lemon peel.

Vodka Espresso

THIS WOULD MAKE A FABULOUS AFTER-DINNER TREAT. IT'S USUALLY
MADE WITH STOLICHNAYA VODKA AND AMARULA, A SOUTH AFRICAN
CREAM LIQUEUR WITH A CARAMEL FLAVOUR.

SERVES 1
cracked ice
2 measures espresso or other
    strong brewed coffee,
    cooled
1 measure vodka
2 tsp caster sugar
1 measure Amarula

1 Put the cracked ice into
    a cocktail shaker, pour
    in the coffee and vodka
    and add the sugar.
2 Cover and shake
    vigorously for 10–20
    seconds, until the
    outside of the shaker
    is misted.
3 Strain into a cocktail
    glass, then float the
    Amarula on top.

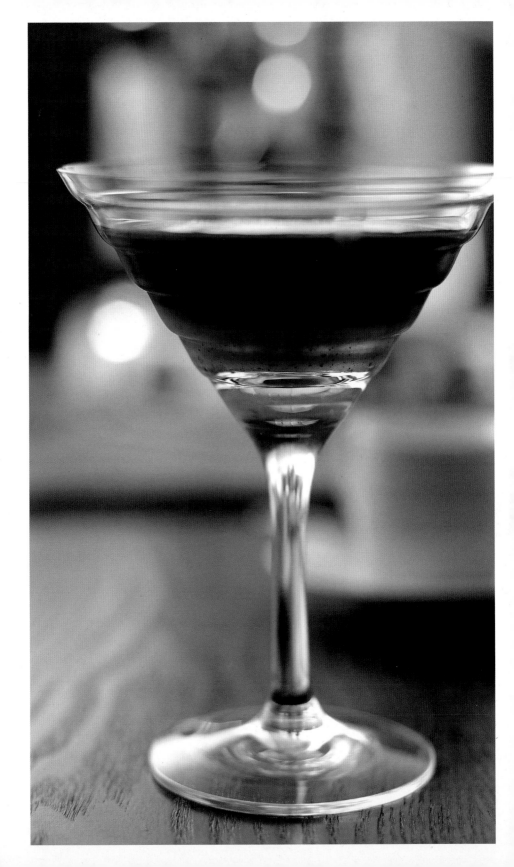

Flying Grasshopper

THERE ARE TWO VERSIONS OF THIS COCKTAIL – ONE MADE WITH EQUAL QUANTITIES OF WHITE AND GREEN CRÈME DE MENTHE, AND ONE WITH GREEN CRÈME DE MENTHE AND CHOCOLATE LIQUEUR.

SERVES 1
cracked ice
1 measure vodka
1 measure green crème de menthe
1 measure white crème de menthe

1 Put the cracked ice into a mixing glass or pitcher and pour in the vodka and crème de menthe. Stir well and strain into a glass.

Flirtini

THIS COMBINATION OF VODKA AND CHAMPAGNE IS GUARANTEED TO
BRINK A SPARKLE TO THE EYES AND A SMILE TO THE LIPS – WHAT COULD
BE MORE ATTRACTIVE?

SERVES 1
¼ slice fresh pineapple,
  chopped
½ measure chilled Cointreau
½ measure chilled vodka
1 measure chilled pineapple
  juice
chilled champagne or sparkling
  white wine, to top up

1 Put the pineapple
  and Cointreau into a
  mixing glass or jug and
  muddle with a spoon
  to crush the pineapple.
2 Add the vodka and
  pineapple juice and stir
  well, then strain into a
  champagne flute.
3 Top up with
  champagne.

Bullshot

THIS IS NOT UNLIKE DRINKING CHILLED CONSOMMÉ – BUT WITH A NOTICEABLE KICK. IT IS BEST REALLY COLD.

SERVES 1
1 measure vodka
2 measures beef consommé
    or good stock
dash fresh lemon juice
2 dashes Worcestershire
    sauce
ice
celery salt
strip of lemon peel, to
    decorate

1 Shake all the liquid ingredients well with ice and strain into a glass with extra ice.
2 Sprinkle with celery salt and dress with the strip of lemon peel.

Cranberry Collins

THE CLASSIC COLLINS DRINK IS MADE WITH GIN, BUT ITS MANY
VARIATIONS ARE MADE WITH OTHER SPIRITS SO TRY THIS ONE FOR SIZE...

SERVES 1
2 measures vodka
¾ measure elderflower
  cordial
3 measures white cranberry
  and apple juice or to taste
ice
soda water
slice of lime, to decorate

1 Shake the first three
  ingredients over ice
  until well frosted.
2 Strain into a glass with
  more ice and top up
  with soda to taste.
3 Dress with the slice
  of lime.

Silver Berry

THIS DRINK IS PERFECT FOR ONE OF THOSE VERY SPECIAL OCCASIONS –
EXCEPT THAT YOU REALLY CAN'T DRINK VERY MANY!

SERVES 1
1 measure raspberry vodka,
  iced
1 measure crème de cassis,
  iced
1 measure Cointreau, iced
frozen berry, to decorate

1 Carefully and slowly
   layer the three liquors
   in the order listed, in a
   well-iced shot glass or
   tall thin cocktail glass.
2 They must be well iced
   first and may need
   time to settle into their
   layers.
3 Dress with the frozen
   berry.

Metropolitan

THIS SOPHISTICATED COCKTAIL FOR CITY SLICKERS SHARES ITS NAME, BUT NOT ITS INGREDIENTS, WITH AN EQUALLY URBANE CLASSIC FROM THE PAST.

SERVES 1
1 lemon wedge
1 tbsp caster sugar
cracked ice
½ measure vodka or lemon
  vodka
½ measure crème de
  framboise or other
  raspberry liqueur
½ measure cranberry juice
½ measure orange juice
2 cranberries, to decorate

1 Rub the outside rim of a glass with the lemon wedge and dip it into the sugar to frost. Set aside.
2 Put the cracked ice into a cocktail shaker and pour in the vodka, liqueur, cranberry juice and orange juice.
3 Cover and shake vigorously for 10–20 seconds, until the outside of the shaker is misted.
4 Strain into the prepared glass, taking care not to disturb the frosting, and decorate with the cranberries.

Party Starter

Tequila Slammer

SLAMMERS ARE ALSO KNOWN AS SHOOTERS. THE IDEA IS THAT YOU POUR THE INGREDIENTS DIRECTLY INTO THE GLASS, WITHOUT STIRRING. COVER THE GLASS WITH ONE HAND TO PREVENT SPILLAGE, SLAM IT ON TO A TABLE TO MIX AND DRINK THE COCKTAIL DOWN IN ONE! DO ENSURE YOU USE A STRONG GLASS!

SERVES 1
1 measure white tequila, chilled
1 measure lemon juice
sparkling wine, chilled

1 Put the tequila and lemon juice into a chilled glass.
2 Top up with sparkling wine.
3 Cover the glass with your hand and slam.

Brain Haemorrhage

THIS IS A RARE INSTANCE OF A COCKTAIL THAT IS DELIBERATELY INTENDED TO LOOK HORRID, RATHER THAN TEMPTING, AND WAS PROBABLY INVENTED TO DRINK AT HALLOWEEN.

SERVES 1
1 measure chilled peach schnapps
1 tsp chilled Baileys Irish Cream
½ tsp chilled grenadine

1 Pour the peach schnapps into a shot glass, then carefully float the Baileys on top. Finally, top with the grenadine.

Toffee Split

YOU SHOULD NOT NEED A DESSERT AS WELL, BUT YOU COULD ALWAYS
POUR THIS OVER SOME ICE CREAM.

SERVES 1
crushed ice
2 measures Drambuie
1 measure toffee liqueur,
    iced

1 Fill a small cocktail
    glass or shot glass with
    crushed ice.
2 Pour on the Drambuie
    and pour in the toffee
    liqueur carefully from
    the side of the glass so
    it layers on top.
3 Drink immediately.

B-52

THE B-52 WAS CREATED IN THE FAMOUS ALICE'S RESTAURANT IN MALIBU, CALIFORNIA. THE NAME REFERS TO THE US B-52 STRATOFORTRESS LONG-RANGE BOMBER.

SERVES 1
1 measure chilled dark crème de cacao
1 measure chilled Baileys Irish Cream
1 measure chilled Grand Marnier

1 Pour the crème de cacao into a shot glass.
2 With a steady hand, gently pour in the Baileys Irish Cream to make a second layer, then gently pour in the Grand Marnier.
3 Cover and slam.

Alabama Slammer

SMALL, BUT PERFECTLY PROPORTIONED – THIS IS A SHOOTER WITH A REAL KICK!

SERVES 1
1 measure Southern Comfort
1 measure amaretto
½ measure sloe gin
½ tsp lemon juice

1 Pour the Southern Comfort, amaretto and sloe gin over cracked ice in a mixing glass and stir.
2 Strain into a shot glass and add ½ tsp lemon juice.
3 Cover and slam.

White Diamond Frappé

THIS IS A CRAZY COMBINATION OF LIQUEURS, BUT IT WORKS WELL
ONCE YOU'VE ADDED THE LEMON. EXTRA CRUSHED ICE AT THE LAST
MINUTE BRINGS OUT ALL THE SEPARATE FLAVOURS.

SERVES 1
¼ measure peppermint
  schnapps
¼ measure white crème de
  cacao
¼ measure anise liqueur
¼ measure lemon juice
ice and crushed ice

1 Shake all the liquid
  ingredients over ice
  until frosted.
2 Strain into a chilled
  glass and add a small
  spoonful of crushed
  ice.

Cowboy

IN MOVIES, COWBOYS DRINK THEIR RYE STRAIGHT, OFTEN PULLING THE CORK OUT OF THE BOTTLE WITH THEIR TEETH. IT IS CERTAINLY DIFFICULT TO IMAGINE JOHN WAYNE OR CLINT EASTWOOD SIPPING DELICATELY FROM A CHILLED COCKTAIL GLASS.

SERVES 1
3 measures rye whiskey
2 tbsp single cream
cracked ice cubes

1 Pour the whiskey and cream over ice and shake vigorously until well frosted.
2 Strain into a chilled glass.

After Five

ORIGINALLY THE NAME OF A MIXED COCKTAIL TOPPED UP WITH
LEMONADE OR SODA, IT HAS NOW BEEN COMPLETELY TRANSFORMED
INTO A LAYERED SHOOTER WITH A REAL KICK.

SERVES 1
½ measure chilled
  peppermint schnapps
1 measure chilled Kahlúa
1 tbsp chilled Baileys Irish
  Cream

1 Pour the peppermint
  schnapps into a shot
  glass. Carefully pour
  the Kahlúa over the
  back of a teaspoon so
  that it forms a separate
  layer.
2 Finally, float the Baileys
  Irish Cream on top.

Layered Lift-Off

Pousse-Café

A POUSSE-CAFÉ IS A LAYERED COCKTAIL OF MANY DIFFERENT COLOURED LIQUEURS. IT IS CRUCIAL TO ICE ALL THE LIQUEURS FIRST.

SERVES 1
¼ measure grenadine
¼ measure crème de menthe
¼ measure Galliano
¼ measure kümmel
¼ measure brandy

1 Ice all the liqueurs and a tall shot, cocktail or pousse-café glass.
2 Carefully pour the liqueurs over a spoon evenly into the glass.
3 Leave for a few minutes to settle.

Aurora Borealis

THIS SPECTACULAR, COLOURED DRINK SHOULD NOT BE MIXED OR STIRRED. LEAVE IT TO SWIRL AROUND THE GLASS, CREATING A MULTI-HUED EFFECT AND TRY TO GUESS THE VARIOUS FLAVOURS.

SERVES 1

1 measure iced grappa or vodka
1 measure iced green Chartreuse
½ measure iced orange Curaçao
few drops iced cassis

1 Pour the grappa slowly round one side of a well-chilled shot glass.
2 Gently pour the Chartreuse round the other side.
3 Pour the Curaçao gently into the middle and add a few drops of cassis just before serving. Don't stir. Drink slowly!

Nuclear Fallout

THIS IS SIMILAR TO A POUSSE-CAFÉ, WHERE THE LIQUEURS ARE
LAYERED, BUT, IN THIS CASE, THE HEAVIEST LIQUEUR IS COLDEST AND
ADDED LAST, TO CREATE THE SLOW DROPPING EFFECT.

SERVES 1
1 tsp raspberry syrup
¼ measure maraschino
¼ measure yellow
   Chartreuse
¼ measure Cointreau
½ measure well-iced blue
   Curaçao

1 Chill all the liqueurs but
   put the blue Curaçao
   in the coldest part of
   the freezer. Also chill
   a shot, pousse-café or
   elgin glass.
2 Carefully pour the
   drinks in layers over
   the back of a teaspoon
   except the blue
   Curaçao.
3 Finally, pour in the blue
   Curaçao and wait for
   the fallout!

Stars and Swirls

YOU WILL NEED A STEADY HAND FOR THIS ONE – PREFERABLY TWO
PAIRS OF STEADY HANDS.

SERVES 1
1 measure Malibu
large ice cube
½ measure strawberry or
    raspberry liqueur
1 tsp blue Curaçao

1 Chill a small shot glass
   really well.
2 Pour in the Malibu and
   add a large ice cube.
3 Carefully pour in the
   other two liqueurs from
   opposite sides of the
   glass very slowly so
   they fall down the sides
   and swirl around.

Fancy Free

THE KEY TO THIS LAYERED DRINK IS TO ICE THE LIQUEUR AND ICE THE GLASS. IF IT DOES SEEM TO MIX ON IMPACT, GIVE IT A LITTLE TIME TO SETTLE AND FORM ITS LAYERS AGAIN.

SERVES 1
⅓ measure cherry brandy, iced
⅓ measure Cointreau, iced
⅓ measure apricot liqueur, iced

1 Pour the three liqueurs in order into an iced elgin, tall shot glass or liqueur glass. Carefully pour them over the back of a spoon so they form coloured layers.

Fifth Avenue

AFTER-DINNER COCKTAILS OFTEN INCLUDE CREAM AND THIS ONE ALSO HAS THE DELICATE FLAVOURS OF APRICOT AND COCOA.

SERVES 1
1 measure dark crème de cacao, iced
1 measure apricot brandy, iced
1 measure cream

1 Pour the ingredients, one at a time, into a chilled tall cocktail glass. Pour the layers slowly over the back of a spoon resting against the edge of the glass. Each layer should float on top of the previous one.

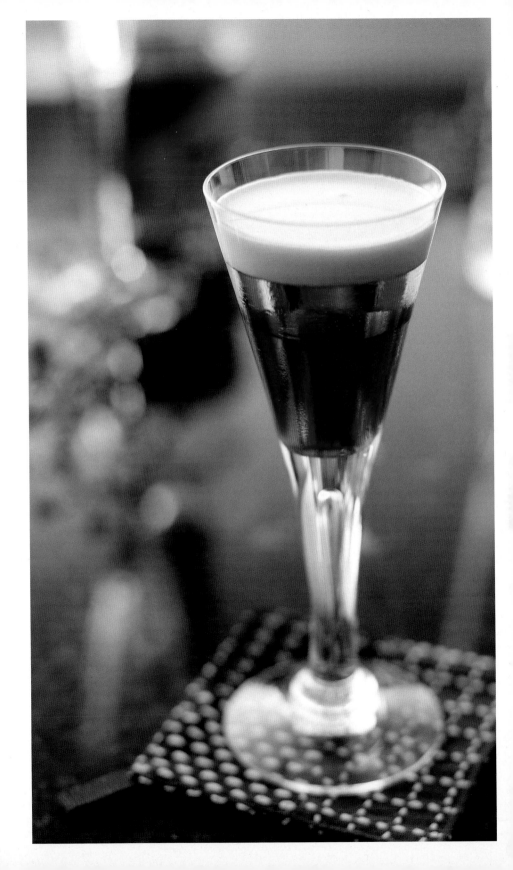

African Mint

AMARULA IS A VERY RICH AND EXOTIC LIQUEUR, WHICH IS BEST SERVED
AND DRUNK REALLY COLD – BUT NOT ON ICE BECAUSE THAT WILL
DILUTE ITS REAL CHARACTER.

SERVES 1

¾ measure crème de
menthe, chilled

¾ measure Amarula, chilled

1 Pour the crème de
menthe into the base
of a shot glass or slim
cocktail glass, saving a
few drops.

2 Pour the Amarula
slowly over the back
of a spoon to create a
layer over the mint.

3 Drizzle any remaining
drops of mint over
the creamy liqueur to
finish.

Napoleon's Nightcap

INSTEAD OF HOT CHOCOLATE, NAPOLEON FAVOURED A CHOCOLATE-LACED BRANDY WITH A HINT OF BANANA. DARING AND EXTRAVAGANT!

SERVES 1

1¼ measures cognac
1 measure dark crème de cacao
¼ measure crème de banane
ice
1 tbsp cream

1 Stir the first three ingredients in a mixing glass with ice.
2 Strain into a chilled cocktail glass and spoon on a layer of cream.

The Perfect Shot

Perfect Love

THIS IS THE LITERAL TRANSLATION FOR AN UNUSUAL PURPLE LIQUEUR FLAVOURED WITH ROSE PETALS, ALMONDS AND VANILLA.

SERVES 1
1 measure vodka
½ measure Parfait Amour
½ measure maraschino
scoop of crushed ice

1 Shake all the liquid
   ingredients together
   over ice until frosted.
2 Strain into a chilled tall
   thin cocktail glass with
   more ice.

Jealousy

THIS REALLY IS AN AFTER-DINNER COCKTAIL AND IF YOU WANT A
CHANGE, YOU COULD OCCASIONALLY FLAVOUR THE CREAM WITH A
DIFFERENT LIQUEUR.

SERVES 1

1 tsp crème de menthe
1–2 tbsp double cream
2 measures coffee or
   chocolate liqueur
crushed ice
chocolate matchsticks, to
   serve

1 Gently beat the mint
   liqueur into the cream
   until thick.
2 Pour the coffee liqueur
   into a very small iced
   glass and carefully
   spoon on the whipped
   flavoured cream.
3 Serve with chocolate
   matchsticks.

Tequila Shot

ACCORDING TO CUSTOM THIS IS THE ONLY WAY TO DRINK NEAT TEQUILA. IT IS OFTEN DESCRIBED AS BEING SMOOTH AND TART, SO ADDING LIME JUICE AND SALT MAY SOUND CONTRADICTORY, BUT IT WORKS!

SERVES 1
1 measure gold tequila
pinch salt
wedge of lime

1 Pour tequila into a shot glass.
2 Put the salt at the base of your thumb, between thumb and forefinger.
3 Hold the lime wedge in the same hand.
4 Hold the shot in the other hand.
5 Lick the salt, down the tequila and suck the lime.

Voodoo

THIS ENTHRALLING MIXTURE OF FLAVOURS IS GUARANTEED TO WEAVE A SPELL ON YOUR TASTE BUDS AND WORK ITS MAGIC FROM THE VERY FIRST SIP.

SERVES 1
½ measure chilled Kahlúa
½ measure chilled Malibu
½ measure chilled
   butterscotch schnapps
1 measure chilled milk

1 Pour the Kahlúa, Malibu, schnapps and milk into a glass and stir well.

Margarita Jelly Shot

IT IS NOT ESSENTIAL TO FROST THE GLASSES WITH SALT BUT IT DOES
LOOK ATTRACTIVE AND PAYS HOMAGE TO THE ORIGINAL NON-JELLY
COCKTAIL RECIPE OF 1942.

SERVES 10
½ lime, cut into wedges
2 tbsp fine salt
1 packet lime jelly
300 ml/10 fl oz hot water
4–5 tbsp Cointreau
200–250 ml/7–9 fl oz tequila

1 Rub the outside rims
  of 10 glasses with the
  lime wedges, then
  dip in the salt to frost
  them. Set aside.
2 Break up the jelly and
  place it in a heatproof
  measuring jug. Pour
  in the hot water and
  stir until the jelly has
  dissolved. Leave until
  cool, then stir in the
  Cointreau and tequila
  to make the mixture up
  to 600 ml/1 pint.
3 Divide among the
  prepared glasses,
  taking care not
  to disturb the salt
  frosting, and chill in the
  refrigerator until set.

Peppermint Patty

SOMETIMES THE SIMPLE THINGS IN LIFE ARE THE BEST – ONE SUCH PLEASURE IS THIS DELICIOUS COMBINATION OF CHOCOLATE AND PEPPERMINT.

SERVES 1
cracked ice
1 measure white crème de cacao
1 measure white crème de menthe

1 Put the ice in a cocktail shaker and pour in the crème de cacao and crème de menthe.
2 Close the shaker and shake vigorously for 10–20 seconds, until the outside of the shaker is misted.
3 Strain into a shot glass or cocktail glass.

Zipper

THIS SHOOTER GETS ITS NAME FROM AN UNUSUAL, NOT TO SAY "LOUCHE" METHOD OF SERVING IT, BUT TASTES JUST AS GOOD SERVED MORE CONVENTIONALLY.

SERVES 1
crushed ice
1 measure tequila
½ measure Grand Marnier
½ measure single cream

1 Put the crushed ice into a cocktail shaker and pour in the tequila, Grand Marnier and cream. Close the shaker and shake vigorously for 10–20 seconds, until the outside of the shaker is misted. Strain into a shot glass.

Index